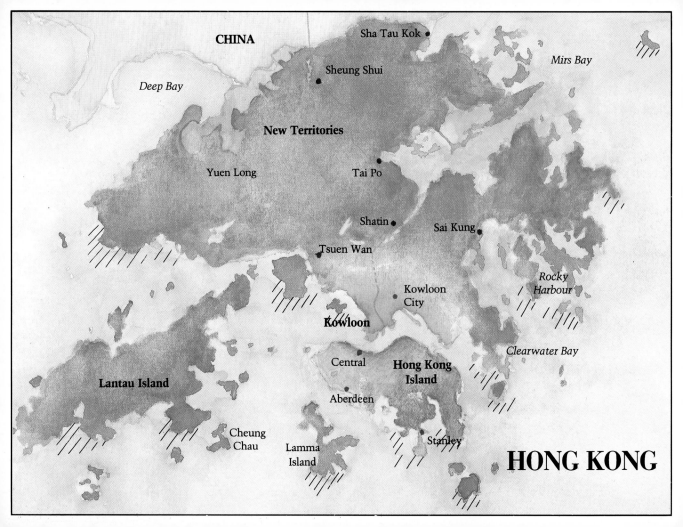

INTRODUCTION

FEW PLACES with as inauspicious a beginning as Hong Kong can lay claim to such great successes. This tiny dot of land situated on the southernmost tip of China, which was once described by a colonial treasurer some 140 years ago as a 'small, barren, unhealthy, valueless island', has managed to overcome an almost complete lack of natural resources to attain an astonishing record of achievement.

Hong Kong was originally developed by the *hongs*, the great British trading companies, as a trading post, an entrepôt port and a meeting place for the exchange of information. Today, however, the colony is this and much, much more. Hong Kong is one of the world's largest manufacturers of garments, toys, radios and watches. Its harbour has just overtaken Rotterdam as the world's most heavily used container port. It is among the world's top 20 financial centres, and after New York and London, undoubtedly the world's third most important business centre. There is business of every variety from billion-dollar syndicate lending to book-keeping, with all the ancilliary legal, insurance, shipping, secretarial, communication, lodging and entertainment services that international commerce today includes.

In addition, Hong Kong boasts one of the world's fastest-growing economies in real terms, it is home to the world's most profitable newspaper, it literally glitters with some of the world's most costly architecture and it possesses some of the world's most renowned hotels.

And of course, Hong Kong's importance as a trading centre has grown with the recent steep rise in economic activity among East and Southeast Asian economies, as the whole region has turned into a thriving marketplace.

But despite a metropolis so modern and prosperous that corporate bonds are available for purchase in underground mass transit stations and Rolls Royces seem as common as taxis, Hong Kong's rural areas still see farmers using water buffalo to plough small plots of land while fishing families spend their whole lives on board floating colonies of *sampans* (small open boats).

The contrasts abound on a cultural level as well. Though its population is nearly 98 percent Chinese, Hong Kong is inundated with seemingly every trapping of Western civilization possible. Yacht clubs, 24-hour supermarkets, and Catholic grammar schools hold their own with *mahjong* parlours (a Chinese gambling game), take-away noodle stands and Buddhist shrines.

In Hong Kong's early days few had any inkling of the successes the 'Fragrant Harbour' (in Chinese 'Hong Kong' means 'fragrant harbour') would some day achieve. In fact, when Britain's emissaries in China seized the single island of Hong Kong from the Manchu Dynasty nearly a century and a half ago, most back in London looked upon the annexation with distinct disfavour.

Though the one responsible for this act — a Captain Charles Elliot — was under instructions from Whitehall to find a 'conveniently situated' island with a harbour close enough to facilitate trade with China (largely in opium), but far enough away to ensure minimum interference, his choice of Hong Kong was met with immediate criticism. Britain's foreign secretary at the time sneered at the potential usefulness of this largely mountainous 'barren island', and even the queen dismissed its worth as a trading centre.

True to the predictions of cynics in London, Hong Kong was initially unable to compete with rich mainland centres such as Shanghai and was an immediate failure as a trading post. For years it foundered as a backwater port brimming with the undesirables of the British Empire — pirates, smugglers and other dubious sorts — all on the alert for illicit profit. In Western eyes Hong Kong did not mean 'Fragrant Harbour' but 'Detestable Society'.

For strategic reasons, however, Britain continued to increase her holdings in the area. Over the next 60 years a portion of the mainland across the water was leased from

Contrasts abound in Hong Kong. Hakka women such as this one wearing traditional tribal headgear make their way between such modern wonders as the gleaming contours of the Far East Finance Centre, a building near Central designed to resemble gold bullion.

China (the tip of this is today known as Kowloon and the areas approaching China are referred to as the New Territories) as well as a host of surrounding islands. It is this 1,050-square-kilometre (405-square-mile) conglomeration of 236 islands and mainland that today make up the British Crown Colony of Hong Kong and that will all be returned to China in 1997.

Today, though the colony's prosperity seems as far-reaching as its concrete and steel studded skyline, uncertainty over what this exchange of sovereignty will mean for the future has already gripped the territory and is marring the confidence economic success would normally bring.

Under an agreement signed in 1984, Hong Kong will be returned to China on 1 July 1997 (the day the 99-year lease on 90 percent of the territory expires) and become a 'Special Administrative Region of China'. On paper, Hong Kong is guaranteed that for 50 years the basic freedoms it now enjoys will be left intact. Beijing has labelled this the 'one country, two systems' formula.

But in Hong Kong, where nearly half the 5.6 million population arrived in the territory after fleeing turbulent upheavals in China, unpleasant recollections of Communist rule do not inspire trust. Some Hong Kong businesses lost their holdings in Shanghai after China went Communist in 1949, and they fear the experience may repeat itself here.

Though Hong Kong has always lived under the onus of 'borrowed time', with many preferring to make their 'pile' quickly before departing to safer shores, the territory suffered its worst bout of jitters during the Sino-British negotiations that led to the 1984 agreement. Stock and property markets plummeted and the Hong Kong dollar took such a beating that the government made a rare exception to its policy of nonintervention and pegged it to the US dollar (at HK$7.80).

Increasingly, however, there are those who believe China will 'let Hong Kong be Hong Kong'. In the last few years, China's operations — at least in the territory — have been determinedly capitalist and there is a growing consensus that the Communist giant really does want to make Hong Kong work.

And it ought to. With the fortunes of nearly one billion people over the barbed-wire fence depending almost as much on Hong Kong as vice versa, many feel China has too much at stake to allow the territory's economy to crumble. Two-thirds of China's foreign investment comes from Hong Kong and 30 percent of its exports pass through the territory. In fact, as China opens more and more to the West, it is helping to direct Hong Kong back to its historic role as an entrepôt, a stopping point for ships in China-Europe trade.

Still, many of Hong Kong's brightest young professionals — foreign-educated doctors, lawyers and bankers — remain unconvinced that Hong Kong's prosperity will continue. They are emigrating to places like the United Kingdom, the United States, Canada and Australia, or salting away their money in foreign banks in case things go sour.

Those who look gloomily at present uncertainty should take heart at the resilience in the face of difficulties that Hong Kong has shown in the past.

In the late 1940s when Hong Kong was very poor and struggling to recover from the ravages of the Second World War, its vulnerable economy was strained by what continues to be both the bane and salvation of the place — its many, many people. In 1949 and in sporadic spurts thereafter, hordes of refugees fleeing China's new Communist regime flooded into the territory. What had been a population of a little over half a million swelled to almost four million by the mid-1960s.

With a mere 30 percent of its land area inhabitable, overcrowding always has been one of the territory's most severe problems. One district in Kowloon is purported to be the world's most densely packed piece of land with 165,000 people crammed like sardines on to each square kilometre. Attempts have been made to alleviate the problem through land reclamation, and approximately 26 square kilometres (10 square miles) has literally been raised from the sea since the colony was created. However, the first influx of refugees in the late 1940s, taking up valuable space, also dramatically changed Hong Kong's fortunes, for it brought a large pool of cheap, hard-working labour with which to begin building the territory's industrial infrastructure of textiles and electronics.

Another event that had an initially destabilising impact was the 1950 United Nations embargo that was placed on trade with China and Korea during the Korean War — a move that all but wiped out Hong Kong's *raison d'être* as an entrepôt. But money and technology from newly immigrated Chinese industrialists were quickly put to use, and the transition from a trading to an industrial economy was so rapid that few people at first realised its significance.

Hong Kong's remarkable resilience and adaptability has continued. When business is slack in one field, Hong Kong wastes no time in switching to another. When the blue jeans fad hit the world in the early 1970s, for example, thousands of denim factories sprouted up all over the territory, but when the market was glutted, many folded as fast as their doors had opened and took advantage of renewed interest in silk.

One root of this flexibility is the traditional Chinese pride of centuries ago when all who were from outside the hallowed borders of the Middle Kingdom were spurned as mere 'barbarians'. It is a pride that reinforces itself, for in order to maintain this sense of superiority, Hong Kong's Chinese must triumph over the odds — and they do.

A more tangible consideration, too, is the lack of a welfare state in Hong Kong. If laid off, a worker cannot wait around for the government to come running to his or her rescue with a handout. Survival means moving on to another job.

Hong Kong's Chinese population runs the gamut from fabulously wealthy industrialists who reside in splendour with servants and Rolls Royces on the Peak (Hong Kong's most prestigious area with breathtaking views of the whole colony) to farmers, fishermen, street-sleepers and shanty town dwellers.

Interspersed among the Chinese are some 168,000 foreigners — the ubiquitous British civil servants, as well as Americans, Australians, Indians, Japanese, Germans and French — most here for just a few years to make themselves richer.

Until the recent implementation of a 'localisation' policy to prepare for the Chinese takeover, it was expatriates who filled the highest positions in government, as well as ran the foreign-owned businesses. And it was expatriates who, simply because of their foreign status, enjoyed privileges far exceeding those doled out to their local counterparts.

But rich or poor, all in Hong Kong seem to share the same penchant for hard work that makes this territory buzz with an energy that never ceases.

It is not uncommon for a person to have two or more jobs. A tailor by day may put away the needle and thread to pick up a toolbox and become an electrician or plumber by night. The official work week is 44 hours, but many in Hong Kong are still going strong for up to 70 hours.

At the height of a working day, the meaning of 'taking it easy', particularly in Hong Kong's main business centre, Central, is seemingly unknown. Legions of pinstripe-suited business people elbow between bare-chested labourers, black-clad grannies, perspiring backpackers and awe-struck tourists. Trams, double-decker buses, taxis, delivery men on bicycles and what is one of the world's highest concentrations of Rolls Royces and Mercedes Benz clog the streets and fill the air with the sounds of motors revving, horns blaring, and bicycle bells clanging.

Just behind this land-lubber's hubbub, the waters of the harbour churn with the traffic of all kinds of vessel. Small craft and large, including ferries, launches, hydrofoils, hovercraft, *sampans* laden with fishing gear, and junks transporting the wealthy out for

While hairstyles may have changed over the years, some things in the territory have not. Chinese junks with sails unfurled still ply the harbour, and sailors from all ports of the world still come here to carouse. Much of Hong Kong has remained immune to the influences of time and the West.

In traditional houses like the one above, tenants read or carry out household chores unperturbed by the lack of windows or the feeble light from an electric bulb. Below effigies of Buddhist and Taoist gods still stand guard in the territory's more than 360 temples.

a floating picnic, all vie for space like toys in a bathtub between massive freighters anchored at their moorings.

It is more than just native industriousness that keeps people going at the pace they do. In this predominantly emigrée society, almost every Chinese who has come here has had to give up a great deal to make that possible. Struggling to regain lost prosperity, or to achieve it in the first place in a society where more rags-to-riches stories abound than even in America, is a constant incentive to hard work in the territory.

Another incentive to hard work is the ease with which a little industry can pay off under a government that takes as little as possible. Hong Kong is run by a governor appointed by Whitehall who presides over an executive council of *ex officio* members (persons who are members by virtue of their official positions) and unofficial members selected by the governor. Laws are enacted by the governor with the advice and consent of a legislative council, with generations of *laissez-faire* principles firmly embedded in its thinking.

Having today the closest approximation to pure capitalist mercantilism to be found anywhere, Hong Kong offers a little bit of the Wild West in the Far East. Virtually anyone can hang out a shingle here with relative ease. Hong Kong's corporate and individual income taxes are among the lowest in the world, it has no import or export duties, it imposes no capital gains tax, and there is no limit to the amount of money that can be transferred in and out of the territory.

The extent to which capitalism thrives in Hong Kong is most evident in its Central business district. Unlike the situation in most of the modern world's great capitals, it is not government buildings that command the most imposing sight in the city but banks — the real power in the territory.

As one approaches Central from the harbour, the towering heights of its many sky-scrapers is a spectacle dazzling enough to make even Dallas look a little faded, but it is the spires of two of the colony's main banks — the Hongkong and Shanghai Banking Corporation and the Bank of China — that dominate the skyline.

The glossy, high-tech heights of the Hongkong Bank, in fact, are not just a testimony to the wonders of modern architecture, but to the bank's wealth — the building is reputedly the most expensive in the world. In 1989 the Bank of China, Beijing's foreign exchange bank, completed their new Hong Kong headquarters. Designed by the Chinese American architect I M Pei, the building towers over the central business district.

No matter how urbane and westernized the exterior of Hong Kong's Chinese, with their English first names and European-cut suits, or the facade of the territory itself with its international restaurants, bilingual media and portraits of Queen Elizabeth II adorning every post-office — Chinese attitudes and some customs remain stubbornly intact.

That Chinese sense of superiority that pushes the individual on in the business world has other manifestations. The conception of the Middle Kingdom's place on the map may have changed, but foreigners are still barbarians and the Chinese still have their inscrutable way of showing it.

Thus the Chinese shopkeeper in Hong Kong will nod and smile ingratiatingly at the unwitting foreigner while at the same time delivering an insult in Chinese. (This derision of foreigners is also a form of psychological defence — after almost a century and a half of foreign domination, lifestyles of Chinese and expatriates are glaringly disparate.)

The rather humourous contempt that the Chinese have for foreigners surfaces in the nickname *gweilo* (literally 'foreign devil') coined for such 'lower' beings. Though the term was originally meant to be derogatory, it has mellowed into neutral slang and even foreigners use it good-naturedly to refer to themselves.

It is also Hong Kong's essential 'Chineseness' that enables a population of nearly six million to survive on this geographic speck of territory. Hong Kong's Chinese seem to have an immunity to noise (radios and TVs are always going full blast) and a penchant for crowds that foreigners find unfathomable. But such 'characteristics' are likely born of the environment. Many in Hong Kong endure conditions so cramped that family members must work and sleep in shifts in order to cope.

One of the most obvious indications of the territory's Chineseness is its dual system of calendars — a system that brings the added benefits of double holidays. Business proceeds along the international solar calendar with holidays such as Christmas, New Year and Easter, but also celebrates the lunar calendar holidays and festivals. It is then that the true spirit of Hong Kong comes through.

The most important holiday on the calendar is Chinese New Year, when houses are brightly lit and red scrolls inscribed with characters signifying happiness, prosperity and long life adorn the walls. Old customs such as bowing in front of elders are revived, as well as the passing out of *lai see*, a red envelope containing lucky money that married couples give to children. No one goes to sleep on lunar New Year's Eve, including small children who are encouraged to keep their eyes open in the belief that it will shorten their lives if they nod off before the advent of the new year.

The Mid-Autumn (*Chung Chiu*) Festival is celebrated on the 15th day of the eighth moon. During this festival everyone eats special 'moon' cakes — a sweet shaped like a crescent and filled with sesame and ground lotus seeds and duck eggs. In addition, the mobile hike out to the hills or open beaches with colourful lanterns for a glimpse of the moon and a shot at having their wishes come true. At night, public parks are spectacular, shimmering with thousands of candlelit lanterns.

There is also the Ching Ming Festival in April when thousands faithfully troop out to ancestral graves to honour their dead with traditional offerings of food and enjoy a family picnic themselves.

Many of the rituals and customs observed in these festivals point to the highly superstitious nature of the Chinese. In fact, superstition finds its way into so many aspects of everyday life that 'superstitious' is probably the closest one can come to naming Hong Kong's predominant religion. Almost every Chinese — whether atheist, Buddhist or Christian — believes in occult forces.

One of the most prevalent manifestations of superstitious belief is the observance of unwritten spiritual laws of geomancy known as *feng shui* that are believed to govern the environment. *Feng shui*, which literally means 'wind and water', is mostly employed in constructing a building in such a way that will bring harmony (and thus it is hoped good luck) to the building's inhabitants. When a new building goes up, a *feng shui* 'consultant' (who, depending on your view of the matter, is either a legitimate scientist or a latter-day voodoo priest) is brought in to assess the proposed site and to offer his highly esteemed (and highly priced) advice on such things as the most propitious place for doors, windows, or even the colour of the walls. Edifices that have benefited from the advice of a *feng shui* consultant include the costly headquarters of the Hongkong and Shanghai Bank (the precise angle of its escalators in fact, were determined by a *feng shui* man), the offices of the *Far Eastern Economic Review*, and one of the territory's newest super-plush hotels, the Regent. *Feng shui* is also employed in choosing grave sites, building roadways and, in earlier times, *feng shui* forests were planted to protect villages.

Then too, there's the preoccupation with lucky numbers. In most places, car owners are more concerned with the letters assigned to their licence plates, but not in Hong Kong. At the periodic 'lucky number' auctions held by Hong Kong's Transport Department, avid seekers of good fortune have forked out as much as US$100,000 for the number of their choice to be attached to their automobile. Lucky numbers include three for 'living or giving birth', six for 'longevity' and eight for 'prosperity'.

Though practically every denomination of the Christian faith is represented in Hong Kong, as well as Islam, Judaism and other Oriental religions, most of Hong Kong's people

The territory's essential 'Chineseness' is apparent in this Taoist mural displayed during a winter solstice festival, in the dark herbal tea dispensed from decorative brass urns and in this turn-of-the-century building located below Hollywood Road.

still practise traditional forms of Chinese worship. Hundreds of Confucian-Taoist-Buddhist temples and shrines are scattered throughout the territory and range from makeshift shrines erected in the home or on the pavement to huge elaborate temples such as the Man Mo Temple on Hollywood Road in Western District or the Temple of Ten Thousand Buddhas in the New Territories town of Shatin.

Millions of tourists enter the territory each year, and while some are just stopping over on the way to China, most come for what Hong Kong itself has to offer.

Many, of course, are lured by the promise of spectacular shopping and bargain buys that arguably top those offered anywhere. There are the hundreds of camera, electronics, optical and jewellery shops that line the Golden Mile strip of Nathan Road on Kowloon side (so named for the seemingly boundless stock of treasures that glitter from display windows). There are factory outlets with cut-rate prices on American, European and local designer clothing scattered everywhere. There are street peddlars seemingly every time you turn the corner, offering fabulous fake Rolex or Cartier watches. There are arty goods galore ranging from expensive water-colours to ridiculously cheap prints, papercuts and cloisonné knick-knacks.

Hong Kong's 20,000 restaurants represent all corners of the globe. They range, of course, from Cantonese or other regional Chinese restaurants to those serving Japanese, Thai, Indian, Malaysian, Korean, Singaporean, or Vietnamese cuisines. Equally impressive is the Continental cuisine to be found in many of the territory's better hotels. And for those who feel they are unable to live without it, American fast food is available on virtually every corner.

Because Hong Kong is essentially a Cantonese city, much of its finest food is Cantonese. Dishes are prepared according to both taste and texture and served with sauces that generally contain contrasting ingredients like vinegar and sugar, or ginger and onion. Delicacies include savoury *dim sum* (Chinese snacks) served in steaming bamboo baskets and selected from trolley carts that make continual rounds between tables, steamed whole fish delicately flavoured with ginger and spring onions, or marvellously crispy-skinned roast suckling pig. Then of course there are the real exotica — dishes made with shark's fin, snake meat, bird's nest, duck webs or deer tails.

Most visitors to Hong Kong confine themselves to the bargain shopping areas of Central and Tsim Sha Tsui, and the obligatory tram ride up to the Peak. Such un-adventurous souls miss out on fully 350 of Hong Kong's 400 square miles and go away feeling Hong Kong is all hustle and bustle and urban environment. A ferryboat out to some of Hong Kong's outlying islands — Lamma, Lantau, Peng Chau or Cheung Chau — and excursions to areas of the New Territories reveal a surprisingly languid side to the territory that should not be missed. Besides being a good opportunity to visit beautiful beaches, see some local Chinese customs — for example the enormous jugs that contain the bones of Chinese dead tucked into hillsides, or Hong Kong's Hakka minority in their native attire — it's a wonderful way to experience the countryside in a relaxing fashion, not often possible elsewhere so close to the city.

This then is a small glimpse of Hong Kong — a territory that in many ways does justice to the epithets coined for it over the years. Hong Kong *can* be considered the Pearl of the Orient, the crossroads of Asia, a bustling port, a shopper's paradise, a concrete jungle, a capitalist bastion, a gourmet's nirvana . . . .

And regardless of the territory's jitters over how the place will change in the future, there are many indications that an even more dynamic plane of activity lies ahead. Ambitious developments costing hundreds of billions of dollars and stretching into the 21st century are planned. These represent an impressive vote of confidence in prospects for the Hong Kong economy and the stability of its society.

Above
Catching a cool breeze and a bit of late afternoon sun makes riding the legendary Star Ferries that crisscross the harbour popular even with the locals. Residents are easily distinguished from tourists, however, as they manage to resist being mesmerised by the constant harbour hubbub and concentrate instead on any of the colony's 68 newspapers or 500-odd periodicals. Hong Kong's flourishing local press includes 44 Chinese-language dailies and two English-language papers. Some of the large Chinese dailies distribute to Chinese communities overseas, and a few even publish editions abroad.

Right
In public parks in the quiet hours of the early morning, locals congregate to practice tai chi ch'uan (chinese shadow boxing). The slow, languid movements of the exercise help to provide a peaceful respite from the pressures of Hong Kong living.

Since 1904, double-decker trams have trundled along what used to be the waterfront linking the western end of Hong Kong island to the east. Besides being a picturesque reminder of an earlier era, trams offer just about the cheapest ride around. A mere 60 cents will allow you to ride from Kennedy Town at one end of the island to Shaukeiwan at the other. In addition, the upper decks of the trams provide one of the best vantage points from which to observe the colony's teeming street life. An end-to-end trip on the tram only covers about eight kilometres but can take as long as two hours.

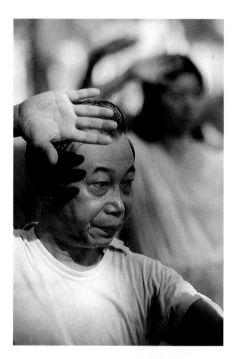

The modernistic headquarters of the
Hongkong and Shanghai Bank, completed
in 1985, is purportedly the world's most
expensive building. Special touches such
as the inclusion of the world's longest
freely supported escalator and an atrium
which rises 52 metres through 11 floors,
helped to push building costs into the
region of HK$5.3 billion.

The green, open slopes of Victoria Peak are
a striking contrast to the dense urban
sprawl of Central's waterfront. Nearly all
this hard ground was once under water.
Reclamation work has been so extensive,
in fact, that engineers once worried that
the changing contours of the shoreline
would affect tidal currents. Hydraulic
research erased any fears, and buildings
have kept popping up with a vengeance.

The Peak Tramway (actually a funicular railway) hauls tourists and commuters up and down Victoria Peak. This is the highest point on Hong Kong island, not just geographically but, with its cool pure air and spectacular views, the coveted retreat of Hong Kong's wealthiest. The actual peak of the Peak is 554 metres (1,828 feet) above sea level.

Left

As aeroplanes take off from Kai Tak, one of the world's few remaining inner-city airports, buildings seem close enough to scrape the plane's underbelly. Traffic at the airport has witnessed rapid growth in the past five years. Kai Tak's single runway, 3,390 metres long, will limit the ultimate capacity of their airport by the 1990s. Several plans for a new airport, entailing civil engineering projects of a mind-boggling scale, have been drawn up by private enterprises. The government has now decided on the island of Lantau as the site for the new airport.

Above

Small but mighty tugboats haul a ship laden with 20- and 40-foot steel containers to berth at Kwai Chung Container Port. Hong Kong recently overtook Rotterdam as the world's leading container port.

Following page

In Hong Kong where utilities, public transport and even airport construction are privatised, it comes as no surprise that the territory is also home to the world's only privately owned and operated container port. Each of Kwai Chung's three terminal operators have constructed all their own facilities, and provided their own equipment — from the gargantuan cranes to the computerised monitoring system.

While most cargo-handling in Hong Kong takes place at the container port, more traditional methods of moving cargo continue. Some 2,000 lighters such as these still draw up to incoming vessels to receive their cargo and bring it to port. The operation of lighters is often a family affair with many serving double duty as floating homes.

This super-developed chunk of land stands where water once lapped against the rocky edge of the Kowloon Peninsula. Known as 'Tsimshatsui East', the segment represents only a small piece of the more than ten miles of land mass that has been vacuumed from the seabed or gouged from mountain sides to help ease the colony's chronic shortage of usable land. Tsimshatsui East's reclaimed foundations now house several luxury hotels, at least a dozen commercial complexes, and most recently the new Hong Kong Cultural Centre and Space Museum.

Rush-hour traffic at the Kowloon entrance to the Cross Harbour Tunnel. Until the middle of the 1970s, the only way for vehicles to cross between Hong Kong Island and Kowloon was on a slow-moving car ferry. With 115,000 vehicles using the tunnel daily (making it the world's busiest four-lane facility), this crossing is anything but quick. Construction on a second tunnel, the Eastern Harbour Crossing, was completed in July 1989 and a third tunnel under the western approaches to the harbour is in the planning stage.

For more than a century, the only way to get to Kowloon from Hong Kong was by Star Ferry. The first Star Ferry was a steam boat that began chugging its way across the harbour in 1870, bearing mainly passengers destined to catch the Orient Express. (The Far East terminus of the train once stood near the Kowloon Star Ferry pier.) Annual passenger traffic in those early years was about 600,000. That same figure is now reached in well under a week. The ten Star Ferries make an average of 455 crossings daily, and during peak hours are packed to the brim with the nearly 600 passengers each can accommodate.

Much of Central's architecture has literally risen from the sea like the glassy spiral of Exchange Square (top and right) which sits on reclaimed land, or the Shun Tak Centre (bottom) from which vessels now leave for Macau. Other buildings have been converted along with the times such as the old ice house of the early 1900s whose storage space is now home to the Fringe Club (centre).

Left
Once one of the most prepossessing structures in Central, the colonial-style Supreme Court Building (which now houses the Legislative Council) is dwarfed by the steely fortress of the Hongkong and Shanghai Bank.

Above
As Hong Kong enters the 1990s, bamboo is still the predominant scaffolding material on the territory's many, many construction sites. Bamboo has characteristics much admired by the Chinese — strength with flexibility. Scaffolders, eschewing safety harnesses and with no fear of heights, scramble all over it like spiders spinning webs.

Right
With a crowd so thick as to obscure most of the goods being sold in this open-air market, it is easy to understand why some parts of Hong Kong are purported to have the highest population density ever experienced by mankind. In the Mongkok district of Kowloon, more than 165,000 people are crammed on to each square kilometre.

These sacks of rice (top) are destined for bins like the ones above or for direct consumption in restaurants. Rice is such an important staple that its various forms have different words: plain rice is mai; cooked rice is faan; rice porridge is juk; and unhusked rice is guk.

Left
Even when not ablaze, neon signs seem to dominate the scene in Hong Kong. The red sign in the foreground is an advertisement for China Products Stores, a string of communist-owned but decidedly capitalistic department stores selling goods from mainland China.

Above
The manufacture of paper offerings is big business in Hong Kong. Designed to resemble traditional money, golden offerings such as these are burned during funerals and various festivals throughout the year to ensure that the dearly departed are well-heeled in the netherworld.

Whether on Hong Kong's super-modern streets where fast-food joints and convenience stores proliferate or here on a back street where tradition still flourishes, much of the colony seems primed for a society constantly in motion. Shops such as this one arrange bowls of tea for quick draining, and even the moments taken to read a newspaper seem stolen from somewhere else. Many in Hong Kong work two or even three jobs with only one weekly rest day.

Besides dispensing tea, Hong Kong's hundreds of herbalists sell traditional remedies for minor ills. Prepared while you wait, cures range from relatively innocuous-sounding dried red dates for gastric disorders, to exotica such as ground deer antler to dried sea-horse or a bit of rhinoceros horn.

Literally meaning 'little heart', dim sum features bite-sized morsels on small plates. To the right is shiu mai, *a steamed dumpling made of minced pork and shrimp.*

Dim sum *includes both sweet and savoury delicacies such as* daan tats, *hot custard tarts.*

Most dim sum, *such as steamed rolls with sweet filling (right), are served in small bamboo steamers.*

Above
Bird aficionados in Hong Kong commonly take their pet songbirds along when they visit their favourite tea house for yum cha. *Tea shops such as this one usually have a rod on which the birdcages can be hung.* Yum cha *is the Chinese version of a tea break featuring various kinds of snacks called* dim sum *(below).*

Right
At least one bird in a handmade cage is a common sight in many Chinese households. The centre for this hobby is a small alley in Kowloon nicknamed 'Bird Street'. Here dozens of dealers sell not just birds, but live grasshoppers and fresh larvae to feed them.

Far right
Indulging in a bit of dim sum is not always a serene affair. Many dim sum restaurants span several floors and during peak times are packed with hundreds of diners all screaming and gesturing for their orders. Dim sum is served from trolley carts pushed through the aisles by serving girls who augment the hullabaloo by chanting traditional rhymes about the food.

All but two percent of Hong Kong's nearly 5.7 million people are Chinese and most have their family origins in Guangdong Province. In line with much of the world, the colony's population is getting older.

Ten years ago, 29 percent of the population was under 15; that figure has now dropped to 23 percent. The proportion of those aged 65 and above has risen from 5.7 percent to eight percent. Males continue to predominate with a current ratio of 1,054 men to every 1,000 women.

More and more modern couples are opting for a Western-style wedding complete with white gown and bouquet. 'Western-style' however, does not necessarily mean 'church wedding'. Last year 45,808 marriages were performed in registries and 2,753 in licensed places of worship. After the legal formalities are done with, a popular place for photograph-taking are the grounds of the Flagstaff Museum of Tea Ware (above).

Traditional wedding ceremonies are still common in Hong Kong, particularly amongst the fishing folk in the New Territories or Outlying Islands. Here the brightly dressed bride and her groom offer tea to their elders as part of the ceremony. According to custom, the elders will at first close their eyes and pretend not to see or hear the couple.

Left
The 60-foot high main temple and the surrounding buildings of Po Lin Monastery on Lantau Island are perhaps the most exquisite examples of traditional Chinese architecture in the colony. In 1990 the work was completed on a giant 35-metre statue of Buddha.

Above
750 metres above sea level and surrounded by mountains, Po Lin Monastery on Lantau Island has about the best location of any of Hong Kong's 360-odd temples and monasteries. Visitors to the monastery can stay overnight in a dormitory — if they can get into the spirit of monastic living and endure the spartan comforts of an extremely hard bed.

Above
Worshippers light joss-sticks at one of the colony's many temples dedicated to Tin Hau, the Goddess of Heaven. Tin Hau is the patron saint of fishing folk — and anyone who comes near the sea including swimmers, surfers and sailors. It is Tin Hau who calms the waters, ensures that the days' catch is bountiful and keeps boats safe from harm.

Right
A priest beats a gong in the Temple of Ten Thousand Buddhas in Shatin, reached by a stiff 500-step climb through pine and bamboo groves. Besides boasting not just ten thousand Buddhas but 12,800, the monastery is home to a nine-storey pink pagoda and mummified priest embalmed in gold leaf. This priest was the monastery's founder who died in 1965, and according to his wishes, was embalmed in a sitting position.

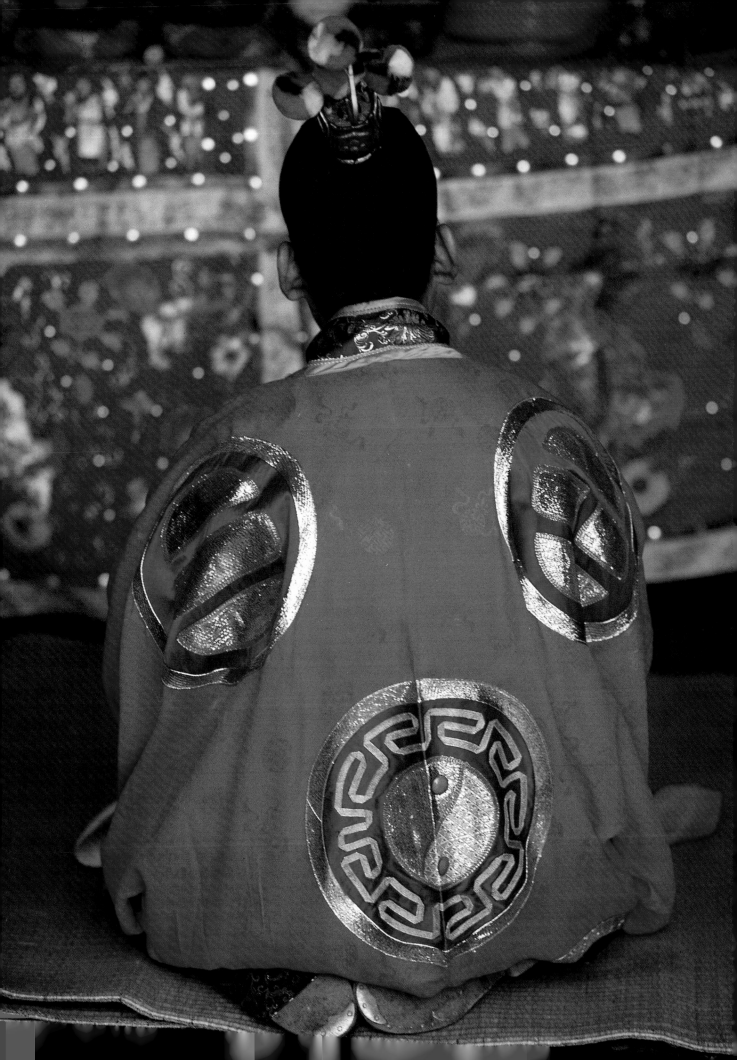

Left
Dressed in a standard red ceremonial robe embellished with the symbols of Yin and Yang, a Taoist priest communes with the gods. It is only after he has put on his ceremonial head covering — the Tung Tin Long Mo *— that the gods will hear his prayers.*

Above
Immense incense coils hang from the ceiling of the Man Mo Temple on Hollywood Road in a section known as the 'smoke tower'. Each coil carries a red tag inscribed with the prayers of worshippers. The coils represent a 'long term' offering as they can burn for up to two weeks. To the left is a stone incinerator for paper offerings.

Above
Celebrating Ta Chiu, the Taoist festival of peace and renewal, in Yuen Long, New Territories. Ta Chiu festivals are held, according to divination, at different times throughout the New Territories; sometimes at an interval of only three years, sometimes as long as 60. The spiritual objectives of Ta Chiu are still considered so important that hundreds of emigrants from overseas return to participate.

Right
Placating the ghosts may be the serious purpose behind this parade staged during the Cheung Chau Bun Festival, but even the most ardent of believers can't keep a straight face all the time. This festival features 60-foot high towers of edible pink and white buns offered first to the ghosts, and later to the living.

Rowing teams of ten to 20 compete in races held throughout the colony in June during the Dragon Boat Festival. Each boat is festooned with a detachable dragon head and tail. As part of the racing ritual, the eyes of each head are dotted with a mixture of red paint and chicken blood to imbue them with a 'live' force. The races are to commemorate an ancient court scholar who committed suicide by hurling himself into a river in protest against the corruption of government officials.

Putting the final touches on a dragon head to be used in a festival parade. Chinese dragons are purely mythical creatures composed of an odd conglomeration of parts of other animals. Among other things, these creatures may sport the head of a camel, the eyes of a hare, the horns of a deer, the scales of a carp, and the paws of a tiger.

Details of the innumerable festivals honouring ghosts or gods staged every year in the territory. As Hong Kong has prospered, festivities have become more elaborate. The 'flower board', right, with its messages of peace and purification was part of a massive Ta Chiu festival costing hundreds of thousands of dollars and shared by many villages.

58

Neat vegetable plots such as these on Lamma Island are generally tilled by hand. Farming is done on a small scale basis in Hong Kong engaging less than two percent of the work force. All vegetable produce is harvested for local consumption (left and right) and constitutes about a third of the vegetables eaten daily. Many farmers often breed ducks on the side.

Above
A Hakka woman tends to her rice paddies in the New Territories. Rice paddies are an endangered species in Hong Kong and increasingly are giving way to vegetable plots. The amount of land devoted to rice cultivation has dropped from over 9,000 hectares in 1954 to less than 10 hectares in 1987. The reason is simple — vegetable production yields higher returns.

Right
Except for the cellophane and the higher price tag of the vegetables (bottom right), all of these pictures show a traditional way of living that still endures. Thousand-year old eggs (top right) have long been a delicacy; farmers have long watered their crops by hand; and fish paste (centre right) has long been dried in the sun in baskets such as these. And hard-working Hakka women have long been the pillars of their matriarchal society.

One of Hong Kong's estimated 24,000 fishermen mending his net. The colony's fishing industry is dominated by the so-called 'boat people' who often spend their entire lives on junks clumped together in congested typhoon shelters. Last year sea-going boat people landed more than 200,000 tonnes of marine fish, most of it going for local consumption.

Boat people in Yaumatei Typhoon Shelter, home to hundreds of fishing families from the Tanka and Hoklo tribes. Historically, neither tribe was accepted by other Chinese and were once barred from living onshore or marrying non-boat people. Today many of these self-sufficient floating communities are shrinking as their young people, no longer facing discrimination, prefer to live on land.

Hong Kong is not just a dichotomy between urban and rural — it also caters to suburban pleasures. The 840-metre roller-coaster above is in Ocean Park which boasts among other things, the world's longest outdoor elevator, the world's largest aquarium, an aviary and a butterfly house. Water World, part of Ocean Park, is a water play park where Hong Kong's youngsters find welcome relief from the oppressive summer heat.

Besides the man-made pleasures afforded by swimming pools, sheltered beaches such as this one in Sai Kung Country Park northeast of Kowloon Peninsula help to make Hong Kong's oven-like summer climate bearable. When temperatures soar well into the 30s, few of the colony's 42 gazetted bathing beaches look as undisturbed as this one.

Hong Kong's 21 country parks reveal a side
to the colony impossible to conceive when
being jostled by crowds in its urban
districts. Country parks cover 40 percent of
Hong Kong's land area and feature
spectacular hill and coastal scenery.
Recreational amenities include picnic and
barbecue facilities, marked hiking paths,
and shelters.

While the Chinese on the other side of the barbed-wire fence may dream longingly of the bright lights of Hong Kong, China can conjure up its own romantic images. This couple sit on a hillside in the New Territories overlooking the Chinese border.

Left
Posters advertising Chinese opera and local cinema attractions. Ever since Bruce Lee propelled Hong Kong films into the limelight, the colony has been a major centre of film-making in Asia. Last year a record 110 films were produced, the majority of which were action features and comedies destined for the local market. While imported films are gaining popularity in Hong Kong, good quality local productions remain the favourite with most cinema-goers.

Right
Traditional Chinese opera is an art that continues to flourish in Hong Kong engaging some 500 full-time actor-singers. Most of the opera performed here is Cantonese, a derivation of the more subdued classical Peking Opera. Costumes are more garish, sets more elaborate, and thoroughly western instruments like electric guitars sometimes replace traditional ones. The roles of Chinese opera were traditionally played by an all-male cast.

The sheer variety of goods displayed in
Hong Kong's shop windows can dazzle
even those who did not set out to buy. As a
duty-free port with only a few commercial
items taxed, Hong Kong is indeed the
bargain basement of the world. Beware of
rampant piratism; Canen is not Canon and
Kolak is not Kodak.

Silk imported from China is both beautiful and expensive, but it is still one of the colony's best bargain buys. Lengths of materials bought may be taken to any of Hong Kong's 4,000 tailors for custom-made tailoring — another of the colony's traditional attractions. Hong Kong's own textile industry produces mainly cotton, most of which is purchased by local clothing manufacturers.

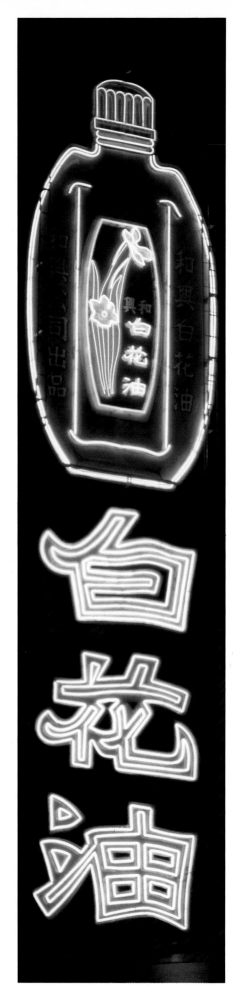

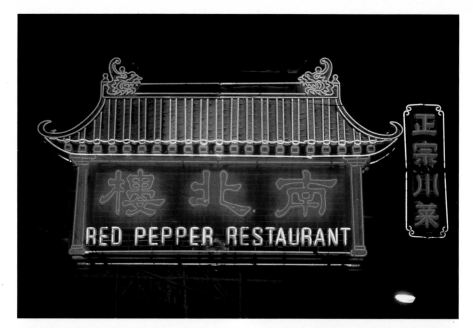

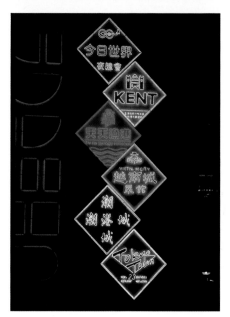

Left

When the sun goes down, the lights come out in Hong Kong. Everything from product advertisements (such as the one for 'White Flower oil' on the left border) to pawn-shop logos (middle right) and even brothel signs (second from bottom on right) vie for attention.

Above

Jumbo is the largest of three floating restaurants located in Aberdeen harbour, home to the colony's largest community of boat people. The three-storey restaurant is reached by sampan and affords a glimpse of the crowded typhoon shelter. Aberdeen's natural harbour once served as an anchorage for early voyagers to China long before the British arrived.

Right

Though the Wild West days of Hong Kong as the stomping ground for sailors and soldiers on R & R is long past, the colony is still a popular port of call. Every year thousands of commercial and military sailors pour into the territory. Some are content with the tawdry girlie bars that line the streets of Wanchai, while others head for the more expensive pleasures of nightclubs (above right).

Left
Fishing off Sai Kung Peninsula.

Above
Picturesque as this quiet harbour with its fishing boats may be, it is likely that the traditional fishing life of Hong Kong's boat people is drawing to a close. Though the amount of fish caught has continued to escalate, the number of working boat people has decreased. As fishing vessels become diesel-powered and thus more expensive to operate and to own, poorer fishing families are driven to shore.

Following page
That well-worn epithet 'capitalist paradise' seems almost forgivable when Hong Kong is unveiled in all its night-time glory — and even without the help of the fireworks. A panorama almost as good as this one can be had from the revolving restaurant at the top of the Hopewell Centre (lower left).

AN A TO Z OF FACTS AND FIGURES

A

Aberdeen Aberdeen is Hong Kong's oldest settlement and today houses the largest floating population in the colony. Approximately 50,000 people live on junks and sampans in the harbour.

Antiques Age is not the only factor to consider when buying Chinese antiques—the quality of work can vary greatly from one dynasty to the next. Fine Chinese bronzes, embroidery and lacquerware may be found throughout the territory, although the main shopping area is Hollywood Road in Central. Buyers should beware of convincing modern imitations!

B

Beaches Swimming is Hong Kong's most popular summer recreation with more than 1.3 million people visiting Hong Kong's 42 beaches. As a consequence many of the strands suffer from pollution. The few remaining unspoilt areas lie in the Sai Kung area of the New Territories.

Brandy Hong Kong is the world's largest consumer of French Cognac. It is loved almost as much for its prestigious price and supposed aphrodisiac qualities as it is for its taste. It is present at every special occasion from business meetings to wedding banquets.

Bride's Pool Bride's Pool is a series of romantic waterfalls in Plover Country Park. The legend behind the name tells of a local girl being carried to her wedding in a sedan chair. Whilst crossing the stream above the waterfall, one of the bearers slipped and tipped the bride over the falls into the pool below. It is said that the ghost of the drowned girl haunts the pool to this day.

Bruce Lee Hong Kong's most famous film export. The martial arts expert kicked his way into his first major role in *Fists of Fury* in 1970. Since his death in 1977 many others have tried to emulate his success. Today's hero is Jacky Chan who enjoys a huge cult following in Hong Kong.

C

Causeway Bay Causeway Bay was originally important because of the large typhoon shelter located there. Today it offers one of the largest shopping areas on Hong Kong Island. Hungry shoppers should look for Food Street which has over 20 restaurants offering both Asian and Western cuisine.

Climate Hong Kong is situated just south of the Tropic of Cancer, resulting in a subtropical climate. In summer the temperature rises to 30°-32°C, with humidity at 90 percent. The best season to visit Hong Kong is autumn when the temperature and humidity drop and days are clear and sunny. From December until February it is moderately cold (average 15°C) and the humidity low. From March to May temperatures vary from 15°-21°C and humidity averages 84 percent.

Cultural Centre The most controversial building in Hong Kong. Despite its choice waterfront location, the building has no windows and no harbour view. It does, however, boast a 2,200 seat concert hall and a host of prestigious arts events.

D

Dai Pai Dong A dai pai dong is a local makeshift restaurant. On average Hong Kong people take one meal a day in a restaurant. The streets are full of 'colourful' but unhygienic cafes, which serve everything from tripe to noodles. For locals who are accustomed to 'sterilising' their cutlery in the glasses of hot tea before eating, this is a quick way to dine.

E

Eight The Chinese believe in numerology and certain numbers are supposed to be particularly significant. The number 'eight' is one of their luckiest numbers since the Cantonese word for 'eight' sounds very much like the word for 'wealth'. The rich hope to ensure safe travel by purchasing number plates for their cars with the number eight on it. These license plates reach staggering prices in government auctions each year.

F

Feng shui Feng shui , which translates as 'wind and water', is the ancient Chinese science of balancing the yin and yang in the natural world. Feng shui experts, called geomancers, are called on to recommend the best site for a building and all the furniture within. Facing water is good feng shui, so properties with no sea view must house water within the building, hence the enormous popularity of aquariums in Hong Kong!

Fanling An important and authentic market place in the New Territories. It is also host to the Royal Hong Kong Golf Club, where international tournaments are held every February. Visitors are welcome to play.

G

Ghurkas This famous British regiment has been serving in Hong Kong since the heyday of the empire. Its members are recruited annually from the hilltribes of Nepal although their future remains uncertain after 1997.

Golden Mile Hong Kong's own special thoroughfare was built through the wilderness of Kowloon by Sir Matthew Nathan, Governor of Hong Kong from 1904 to 1907. Formerly known as Nathan's Folly, the Golden Mile today is full of glittering hotels, restaurants and constant shopping crowds.

H

Hungry Ghosts Festival The Yue Lan or Hungry Ghosts Festival takes place on the 15th day of the Seventh Moon which usually falls in September. The festival takes place to placate those ghosts that have become dispossessed and who may return to wreak havoc. Offerings are made in the form of paper replicas of material possessions such as cars, houses, food and 'money'. These replicas are burnt and allow the disgruntled ghosts to return happily to heaven laden with their new-found wealth.

I

IIs Illegal Immigrants, or IIs as they are locally known, come in their thousands across the hilly Chinese border each year looking for work in Hong Kong. Many are caught by the authorities during spot checks on MTR stations and building sites, when employees are asked to produce their Hong Kong identity cards.

J

Jade Market Situated on Gascoigne and Battery Streets in Yau Ma Tei are 450 registered jade stalls. The jade comes in all shapes and colours from Burma, China, Australia and Taiwan. The Chinese wear the stone as a protection against disease and evil. It is also a symbol of beauty, nobility and purity.

K

Kam Tin Kam Tin is situated on the western side of the New Territories and houses three traditional walled villages. The largest of these is Kat Hing Wai and dates back some four or five centuries. The village is square and completely surrounded by brick walls as protection against bandits and pirates. The Tang clan were the first to establish themselves here and their descendants inhabit the village to this day.

L

Lok Ma Chau Hongkong's lookout over China. For the best view of China, travel up the hill, off Lok Ma Chau Road, and look out across the meandering Shenzen River, paddy fields and duck ponds.

Ling Ling Cha Cha Dum Dum Sai Translated literally means 'Bells sound, cymbals crash everything is disaster' and is the Cantonese way of summing up a bad meal. Fortunately it is rarely used.

M

Mai Po Marshes One of the most important sites for wildlife in Hong Kong. A restricted area, it is managed by the Worldwide Fund for Nature. Its 380 hectares (938 acres) of mudflats, shrimp ponds and mangrove swamps are home to more than 250 species of birds and is an internationally significant site for migratory birdlife.

The Middle Kingdom The Middle Kingdom is a multi-million dollar entertainment centre, located in Ocean Park. It offers a potted history of China through a variety of exhibitions, plays and martial arts displays.

N

Noon Day Gun The Noon Day Gun sounds every day over the harbour in Causeway Bay. It was immortalized by Noel Coward: 'In Hong Kong they strike a gong and fire off a noon day gun, But mad dogs and Englishmen go out in the midday sun.'

Newspapers Hong Kong boasts more than 34 Chinese dailies and four English newspapers—*The South China Morning Post, The Hong Kong Standard, The Asian Wall Street Journal* and *The International Herald Tribune.*

O

Opera Cantonese Opera is an ancient art that is poorly paid and hard work. Its appeal lies in its representation of archetypal characters and qualities such as virtue, corruption, youth, age, violence and lust. Over the years it has been used as a medium for criticism of officialdom in the guise of harmless fun. Amateur performances can be seen each night in Temple Street.

P

Poor Man's Night Club A car park by day, the Poor Man's Night Club appears magically each night, selling everything from cassettes, records and electronic gadgets to seafood and noodles—it is located near the Macau ferry terminal.

Q

Qigong Qigong is an ancient Chinese breathing exercise that has enjoyed a resurgence in recent years. A great deal of research has been conducted to discover the secret of this psychic art, which is said to cure diseases such as cancer.

R

Religion All the religions of the world can be found in Hong Kong and are practiced with complete freedom. Buddhist monasteries and Taoist temples coexist with Christian churches, Muslim mosques, and Hindu and Sikh temples.

S

Sha Tin Racecourse Built at a cost of HK$60 million, Sha Tin is the place for high-tech gambling. Punters can place their bets using state-of-the-art computers and watch the race in close-up on the giant infield video screen.

Snake Soup Served with chrysanthemum flowers, snake soup is a heart-warming winter dish. The gall bladder can also be removed and added to a glass of wine as a cure for arthritis or as a general stimulant.

T

Telephones Telephone calls within Hong Kong are free and telephones are readily available in corner shops, stores and restaurants. Despite their availability, the portable phone has found great popularity with the Yuppy community and proud owners can be seen ostentatiously flourishing their pieces on streets throughout Hong Kong.

Timepieces Hong Kong exports more clocks and watches than Switzerland. Famous name watches can be bought from both reputable dealers and from extremely disreputable hawkers on Nathan Road. Buyers should note however, that the imitation's life span is usually directly related to the price paid.

U

Undeveloped Little of Hong Kong remains undeveloped. In fact much of the urban landscape has been moulded by the removal of hills! These have been used as landfill for the various reclamation sites to be found throughout the territory.

V

Victoria Peak Rising steeply from the harbour, the Peak offers a superb 360° view of Hong Kong. It is best approached by the Peak Tram which runs from Garden Road in Central. On reaching the Peak, energetic visitors can enjoy a walk along one of the paths that wind their way around the hill.

W

Walla-Wallas Walla-wallas are the motorized sampans which can be seen chugging across the harbour. Nobody seems to know exactly why they have such a peculiar name. Some say it's the sound that they make, while others suggest it is the name of the first of its kind owned by a man from Wala Wala, Washington, USA.

Wong Tai Sin One of the most popular and 'luckiest' temples in Hong Kong. At Lunar New Year, local celebrities queue up with the masses to have their fortune told.

X

Exotica The Cantonese are said to eat everything that flies in the air, swims in the sea or walks on the land. Some restaurants cater to such whims with such specialities as bear's paw, civet and lichen.

Y

'Yue People' Little is known of Hong Kong's prehistory, but ancient Chinese literary records speak of a maritime people who occupied China's southeastern seaboard and were known as the Yue. It is probable that Hong Kong's prehistoric inhabitants belonged to 'The Hundred Yue', as this diverse group of people is often called.

Z

Zoological and Botanical Gardens Situated at the foot of Victoria Peak and overlooking Government House, the Zoological and Botanical Gardens contain a wide variety of flora and fauna. The mammal collection includes orang utans and tamarins while the bird collection is one of the best in Asia. The gardens are a popular spot for early morning devotees of tai chi chuan—an ancient form of Chinese exercise.

INDEX

GS/02/04